TWO TRUTHS AND A MYTH

Tutankhamun's TOMB

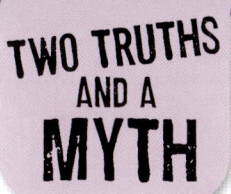

SPOT THE MYTHS

by Carol Kim

a Capstone company — publishers for children

Raintree is an imprint of Capstone Global Library Limited, a company incorporated in England and Wales having its registered office at 264 Banbury Road, Oxford, OX2 7DY – Registered company number: 6695582

www.raintree.co.uk
myorders@raintree.co.uk

Hardback edition text © Capstone Global Library Limited 2025
The moral rights of the proprietor have been asserted.

All rights reserved. No part of this publication may be reproduced in any form or by any means (including photocopying or storing it in any medium by electronic means and whether or not transiently or incidentally to some other use of this publication) without the written permission of the copyright owner, except in accordance with the provisions of the Copyright, Designs and Patents Act 1988 or under the terms of a licence issued by the Copyright Licensing Agency, 5th Floor, Shackleton House, 4 Battle Bridge Lane, London, SE1 2HX (www.cla.co.uk). Applications for the copyright owner's written permission should be addressed to the publisher.

Editorial credits
Edited by Carrie Sheely
Designed by Bobbie Nuytten
Media Research by Rebekah Hubstenberger
Production by Whitney Schaefer
Originated by Capstone Global Library Ltd

ISBN 978 1 3982 5656 9 (hardback)

British Library Cataloguing in Publication Data
A full catalogue record for this book is available from the British Library

Acknowledgements
We would like to thank the following for permission to reproduce photographs: Alamy: Barry Iverson, 18, Danita Delimont, 25, North Wind Picture Archives, 9, The Print Collector, 7; Associated Press: Amr Nabil, 13; Getty Images: Brandon Rosenblum, 23, Culture Club, 4, Grafissimo, 8, Historica Graphica Collection/Heritage Images, 21 (top), Hulton Archive, Cover, 14, 28, Khaled DESOUKI/AFP, 26, Scott Olson, 29, Universal History Archive/Universal Images Group, 17; Newscom: imageBROKER/Raimund Franken, 13; Shutterstock: Apostrophe, design element (texture), Everett Collection, 11, Jaroslav Moravcik, 21 (bottom right), Tasha Romart, design element (icons); The Metropolitan Museum of Art: Purchase, Edward S. Harkness Gift, 1926, 22

Every effort has been made to contact copyright holders of material reproduced in this book. Any omissions will be rectified in subsequent printings if notice is given to the publisher.

All the internet addresses (URLs) given in this book were valid at the time of going to press. However, due to the dynamic nature of the internet, some addresses may have changed, or sites may have changed or ceased to exist since publication. While the author and publisher regret any inconvenience this may cause readers, no responsibility for any such changes can be accepted by either the author or the publisher.

Printed and bound in India.

CONTENTS

A tomb of treasures **4**

The boy king **6**

The tomb **10**

The discovery **14**

The mummy **18**

Death of the king **22**

The artefacts **26**

Glossary 30
Find out more 31
Index 32
About the author 32

Words in **bold** are in the glossary.

A tomb of treasures

Tutankhamun was an ancient Egyptian king, or pharaoh. For more than 3,000 years, his tomb lay undisturbed deep underground. That changed when English **archaeologist** Howard Carter uncovered the tomb in Egypt's Valley of the Kings in 1922.

The remarkable treasures found in Tutankhamum's tomb made him a famous pharaoh. But he was not well known before his tomb was discovered.

A sculpture of Tutankhamun's head was found in the entrance to the pharaoh's tomb.

Scientists have closely studied Tutankhamun and his tomb for more than 100 years. But people continue to believe many myths about them. Read along to explore the facts and myths. Three statements will be presented together. One is a myth or **misconception**. Can you separate the myth from the facts?

HOW CAN I TELL WHAT'S TRUTH AND WHAT'S A MYTH?

START HERE. ⇨ Does the statement include words like "all" or "none"?

YES ⇨ It might be a myth. Words such as "all" or "none" often simplify complicated topics. These statements might not be true.

NO ⇨ Does the statement include specific information, such as names or dates?

YES ⇨ It might be true. Details are important when dealing with facts. The more details a statement provides, the more likely it is to be true.

NO ⇨ It might be a myth. Vague facts without detail might be made up. It's good to question statements that don't include specific details.

The boy king

TRUTH OR MYTH?

1. TUTANKHAMUN DID LITTLE DURING HIS REIGN THAT HAD ANY LONG-TERM EFFECTS ON EGYPTIAN LIFE.

Tutankhamun was Egypt's ruler for a relatively short amount of time – about 10 years. His father, Akhenaten, was pharaoh for 17 years. Some pharaohs ruled for much longer. Tutankhamun's short reign affected how much he was able to accomplish. It didn't have lasting effects.

2. TUTANKHAMUN WAS ONLY 9 YEARS OLD WHEN HE INHERITED THE THRONE.

Tutankhamun was born around 1341 BCE. Akhenaten died in 1336 BCE. Tutankhamun was just a young boy. At the time, his name was Tutankhaten. He took over as king when he was 9 years old.

3. LEADERS WHO CAME AFTER TUTANKHAMUN REMOVED HIS NAME FROM MANY OFFICIAL RECORDS. HE WAS ALMOST FORGOTTEN UNTIL THE DISCOVERY OF HIS TOMB.

Before the reign of Akhenaten, Egypt had been a very rich and powerful country. But while Akhenaten was king, it began to show signs of decline.

For hundreds of years, Egyptians worshipped many gods. When he became king, Akhenaten allowed people to worship only the sun god Aten. He also moved the capital from Thebes to Amarna.

Akhenaten

Rulers who came after Tutankhamun believed that Akhenaten's changes had had a bad effect on Egypt. They tried to erase Akhenaten from history as well as his son, Tutankhamun. Their names were removed from official lists of kings. Tutankhamun's name was even chiselled off all his statues.

THE MYTH

TUTANKHAMUN DID LITTLE DURING HIS REIGN THAT HAD ANY LONG-TERM EFFECTS ON EGYPTIAN LIFE.

After the death of his father, Tutankhamun was aware of how unpopular some of his father's actions had been. He reversed many of his father's changes. He allowed people to worship many gods again. He moved the capital back to Thebes. Temples and palaces were rebuilt. His decisions helped rebuild Egypt's **economy**.

A pharaoh and other ancient Egyptians worship the god Sobek.

The Karnak temple complex in Thebes was an important religious centre of ancient Egypt.

The tomb

TRUTH OR MYTH?

1. TUTANKHAMUN'S TOMB IS SMALLER THAN THOSE OF OTHER PHARAOHS.

The thousands of items in Tutankhamun's tomb included clothes, jewellery, large furniture pieces and six **chariots**. But the tomb is small for a pharaoh. Tutankhamun may have died unexpectedly. It is possible that there wasn't time to prepare a larger tomb.

2. THERE ARE SECRET ROOMS IN TUTANKHAMUN'S TOMB THAT HAVE NOT YET BEEN UNCOVERED.

In 2014, the wall surfaces inside Tutankhamun's tomb were scanned. Egyptologist Dr Nicholas Reeves studied the images. He suggested that the images showed outlines of sealed doorways that led to hidden rooms. He also said Egyptian queen Nefertiti could be buried in one of the hidden rooms.

3. TUTANKHAMUN'S TOMB IS MADE UP OF FOUR ROOMS AND A CORRIDOR. THE ROOMS ARE AN ANNEXE, ANTECHAMBER, TREASURY AND BURIAL CHAMBER.

After going down the steps to the first door, there is a corridor that leads to a second door. It opens to the antechamber. It is the first room filled with treasures. The next room is the annexe. The burial chamber is where the remains of Tutankhamun were found. The treasury was filled with many items, including his **embalmed** organs.

Artefacts from Tutankhamun's tomb

FACT

More than 5,000 objects were dug out from Tutankhamun's tomb.

THE MYTH

THERE ARE SECRET ROOMS IN TUTANKHAMUN'S TOMB THAT HAVE NOT YET BEEN UNCOVERED.

Between 2015 and 2018, people did three more scans of the tomb walls. In 2018, 40 scans were taken. Most experts decided that the scans did not show any **evidence** of hidden rooms. Dr Reeves later said he may still be correct. But most experts do not agree.

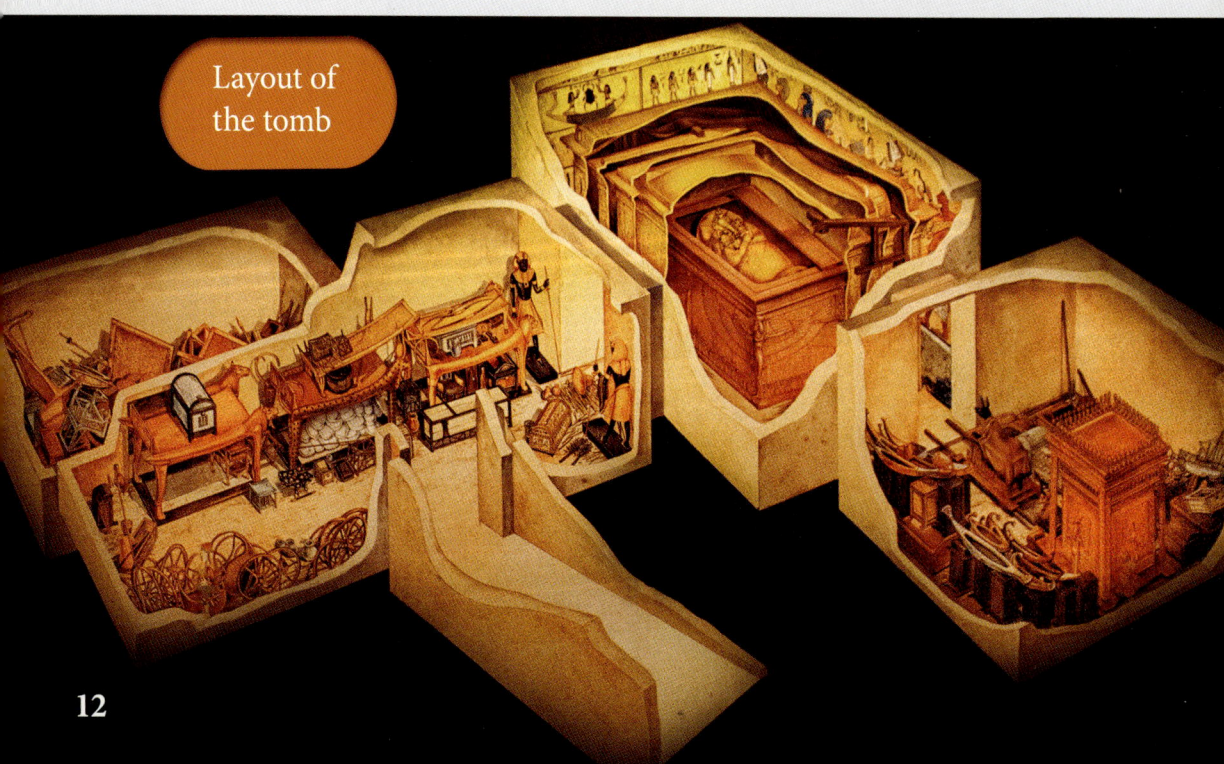

Layout of the tomb

An expert scans a wall in the tomb's burial chamber in 2016.

The discovery

TRUTH OR MYTH?

1. HOWARD CARTER WAS THE FIRST TO DISCOVER THE STEPS THAT LED TO THE TOMB.

Howard Carter had a team of local Egyptian workers helping him search for Tutankhamun's tomb. They had to clear lots of rock and debris.

Lord Carnarvon was Carter's sponsor. He provided the money for the search. In October 1922, Carnarvon was ready to give up the search. But Carter convinced him to keep going.

Carter and his team worked even harder. In November, Carter discovered the tomb steps by chance.

Howard Carter (right) walks alongside Lord Carnarvon in the Valley of the Kings in 1922.

2. AFTER UNCOVERING THE STEPS TO THE TOMB, CARTER HAD TO COVER THEM UP AND WAIT FOR LORD CARNARVON TO ARRIVE.

Carter and his team dug until they uncovered 16 steps and reached the top part of a door.

At that point, Carter reburied the door and steps. He sent a message to Carnarvon, telling him of the discovery. Then he had to wait. It took more than two weeks for Carnarvon to travel to Egypt. After he arrived, Carter was able to start digging again.

3. HOWARD CARTER WAS NOT THE FIRST TO ENTER TUTANKHAMUN'S TOMB SINCE HIS BURIAL.

Howard Carter was the first person to uncover Tutankhamun's tomb in modern times. As he dug, he saw signs that robbers had entered the tomb earlier. The signs suggested that robbers had broken in not long after Tutankhamun's burial.

Carter discovered that the upper-left corner of the door to the tomb had been opened and resealed at least twice. Fortunately, the robbers had not gone further than the antechamber.

THE MYTH

HOWARD CARTER WAS THE FIRST TO DISCOVER THE STEPS THAT LED TO THE TOMB.

Howard Carter had a team of workers helping him search for Tutankhamun's tomb. Some historians believe it was the team's water boy, Hussein Abd el-Rassul, who discovered the staircase. Carter was not even at the dig site at the time.

Some stories say that, on the morning of 4 November 1922, Hussein took jars of water to the workers. While placing the jars in the sand, his hand brushed against some stone. Looking closer, he found the top of a step cut into the ground. When Carter arrived later, the workers were waiting to show him what Hussein had found.

Hussein Abd el-Rassul wears a necklace from the tomb.

The mummy

TRUTH OR MYTH?

1. HOWARD CARTER HAD TO REMOVE TUTANKHAMUN'S BODY FROM THE COFFIN IN PIECES, INCLUDING CUTTING THE HEAD OFF AT THE NECK.

As part of the burial process, oils had been poured all over Tutankhamun's body. The oils had hardened. They kept his body firmly glued inside. Howard Carter tried to soften the sticky layer, but nothing worked.

He had no choice but to remove the mummy from the coffin in pieces. His team had to cut the head off at the neck. They also separated the pelvis from the trunk and detached the arms and legs.

Tutankhamun's mummy

2. TUTANKHAMUN'S MUMMY CAUGHT FIRE AFTER HIS BURIAL.

Egyptologist Chris Naunton studied some remains of Tutankhamun under a powerful microscope. There were signs that the remains had been burned. He believed the embalming oils had produced a chemical reaction. This caused the mummy to catch fire.

3. A "MUMMY'S CURSE" WAS BEHIND THE DEATHS OF SEVERAL PEOPLE INVOLVED IN OPENING TUTANKHAMUN'S TOMB.

Lord Carnarvon died less than five months after opening Tutankhamun's tomb. Soon, people began saying his death was caused by a "mummy's **curse**".

Some newspapers reported that a curse was found written on a clay tablet just outside the tomb. Other reports said more than 12 mysterious deaths could be linked to the curse. They included Lord Carnarvon's half-brother Aubrey Herbert and a wealthy railway executive called George Jay Gould. Both deaths took place within a year after the tomb's discovery.

THE MYTH

A "MUMMY'S CURSE" WAS BEHIND THE DEATHS OF SEVERAL PEOPLE INVOLVED IN OPENING TUTANKHAMUN'S TOMB.

Stories of a written curse turned out to be untrue. Reporters had spread rumours of a supposed curse to stir up the interest of readers.

The deaths said to be linked to the mummy's curse were not from mysterious causes. Lord Carnarvon cut a mosquito bite on his face with a razor. The cut developed into a blood infection, which led to his death. Carnarvon had also been in poor health for years.

Only six of the 26 people who were at the tomb's opening had died within 10 years. Howard Carter lived for another 17 years.

Lord Carnarvon leads a group of people invited to the unofficial opening of Tutankhamun's tomb.

FACT

A guard watching over Tutankhamun's funerary mask on display in San Francisco, USA, claimed he had had a mild stroke because of the "mummy's curse". He tried to get payment for his health issue. But a judge threw out the claim.

Death of the king

TRUTH OR MYTH?

1. TUTANKHAMUN WAS MURDERED BY A BLOW TO THE HEAD.

In 1968, researchers took an X-ray of Tutankhamun's mummy. They found some small bone fragments inside his skull. It showed that Tutankhamun had been killed by a blow to the back of his head.

2. TUTANKHAMUN WAS BURIED WITH SMALL FIGURINES MEANT TO ACT AS SERVANTS IN THE AFTERLIFE.

Ancient Egyptians believed in an afterlife. Tutankhamun's tomb included hundreds of small figurines called shabtis. Carved into some of the figures was a magical spell. It told a shabti to work for the king in the afterlife.

Shabti

3. THE TOMB WAS PREPARED IN A HURRY AND SEALED BEFORE THE PAINT WAS DRY ON THE WALLS.

Tutankhamun's death may have taken everyone by surprise. Usually the tombs of pharaohs took many years to prepare. But for Tutankhamun, many items had not been crafted yet.

There are spots of mould on the painted walls inside the tomb. The mould formed because the paint was not yet dry when the tomb was sealed. This helps to prove that the burial was rushed.

The painted walls of Tutankhamun's burial chamber show his journey into the afterlife.

THE MYTH

TUTANKHAMUN WAS MURDERED BY A BLOW TO THE HEAD.

In 2005, experts performed a CT scan of Tutankhamun's mummy. These scans produce more detailed images than X-rays. The scan proved that the skull damage happened after his death. It was either caused during the mummification process or when Howard Carter removed Tutankhamun from his coffin.

FACT

Experts believe the most likely cause of Tutankhamun's death was either an infection from a broken leg or malaria. Malaria is a disease that can be given to people by mosquitoes.

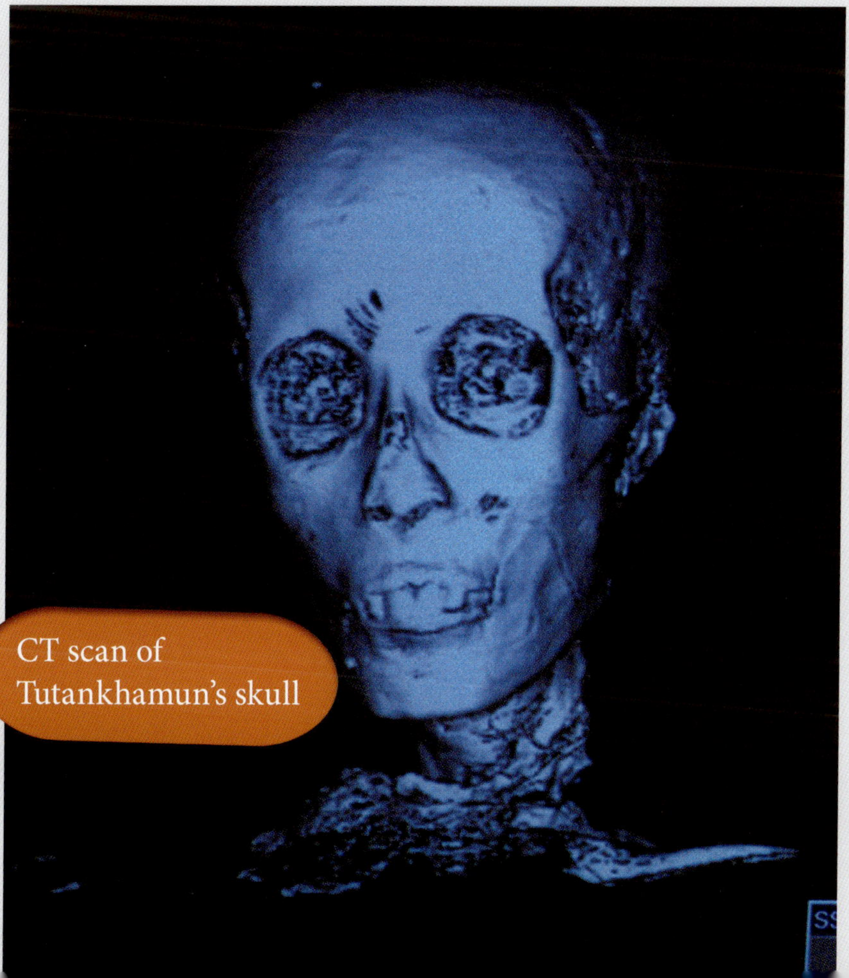

CT scan of Tutankhamun's skull

The artefacts

TRUTH OR MYTH?

1. IMAGES OF TUTANKHAMUN'S ENEMIES WERE ON THE SOLES OF HIS SANDALS. ANCIENT EGYPTIANS THOUGHT THIS WOULD ALLOW HIM TO STEP ON THE FACES OF HIS ENEMIES WHENEVER HE WALKED IN THE AFTERLIFE.

The **artefacts** in the tomb included at least 80 pairs of footwear. The soles of some sandals had images of Tutankhamun's enemies.

Copies of sandals found in Tutankhamun's tomb

2. ROBBERS WERE THE ONLY ONES TO TAKE ITEMS FROM TUTANKHAMUN'S TOMB AFTER HIS BURIAL.

Items were almost certainly taken from Tutankhamun's tomb by robbers 3,000 years ago. But no evidence was found that anyone besides the robbers took anything.

3. AN IRON DAGGER WAS FOUND IN THE TOMB STRAPPED TO TUTANKHMANUN'S BODY. THE IRON COULD HAVE COME FROM A METEORITE.

An iron dagger was found in the fabrics wrapped around Tutankhamun's body. But Egyptians did not begin to work with iron metal for another 500 years.

So how did Tutankhamun come to have an iron dagger? Experts think it may have been a gift from a king outside of Egypt. One possible source was a meteorite. Meteorites are pieces of space rock that reach Earth. They often contain iron.

THE MYTH

ROBBERS WERE THE ONLY ONES TO TAKE ITEMS FROM TUTANKHAMUN'S TOMB AFTER HIS BURIAL.

There is strong evidence that Howard Carter took some items from Tutankhamun's tomb during the **excavation**. One object is an **amulet** Carter gave to Sir Alan Gardiner, a member of the excavation team, in 1934. Carter claimed it was not from the tomb. But a member of the Egyptian Museum in Cairo said that it perfectly matched other objects from Tutankhamun's tomb. Experts think it's likely that Carter didn't think it was wrong to take some small items and give them as gifts.

Howard Carter

More than 100 years ago, the world was amazed at the discovery of Tutankhamun's tomb. From this famous find grew many myths. How many myths did you spot?

A small coffin in the tomb held Tutankhamun's mummified liver.

GLOSSARY

amulet small charm believed to protect the wearer from harm

archaeologist person who learns about the past by digging up old buildings or objects and studying them

artefact object made by human beings, especially a tool or weapon used in the past

chariot two-wheeled fighting platform used in ancient times that was usually pulled by a horse

curse evil spell meant to harm someone

economy ways in which a country handles its money and resources

embalm preserve a dead body so it does not decay

evidence information, items and facts that help prove something to be true or false

excavation process of digging something out

misconception wrong or inaccurate idea

FIND OUT MORE

BOOKS

The Curse of the Mummy: Uncovering Tutankhamun's Tomb, Candace Fleming (Scholastic, 2024)

The Story of Tutankhamun, Patricia Cleveland-Peck (Bloomsbury, 2017)

Tutankhamun's Tomb (I Was There), Sue Reid (Scholastic, 2020)

WEBSITES

www.bbc.co.uk/bitesize/articles/zvmkhbk
Discover more about Tutankhamun with BBC Bitesize.

www.beano.com/posts/tutankhamun-facts
Find out more facts about Tutankhamun on the Beano website.

www.natgeokids.com/uk/discover/history/egypt/tutankhamun-facts/
The National Geographic Kids website has lots of fascinating facts about Tutankhamun.

INDEX

Abd el-Rassul, Hussein 16, 17
afterlife 22, 23, 26
Akhenaten 6, 7
annexe 11
antechamber 11, 15

burial chamber 11, 13, 23

Carter, Howard 4, 14, 15, 16, 18, 20, 24, 28
CT scans 24
curses 19, 20, 21

fire 19

gods 7, 8

hidden rooms 10, 12

iron daggers 27

Lord Carnarvon 14, 15, 19, 20, 21

oils 18, 19

robbers 15, 27, 28

sandals 26
shabtis 22
steps 11, 14, 15, 16

Thebes 7, 8, 9
treasury 11

X-rays 22, 24

ABOUT THE AUTHOR

Carol Kim is the author of several fiction and non-fiction books for children. She enjoys researching and uncovering little-known facts and sharing what she learns with young readers. Carol lives in Austin, Texas, USA, with her family. Learn more about her and her latest books at her website, CarolKimBooks.com.